THE BRITISH SOLDIER IN THE 20TH CENTURY

Written and illustrated by

MIKE CHAPPELL

WESSEX MILITARY PUBLISHING

First published in the United Kingdom in 1990
by Wessex Military Publishing

ISBN 1 870498 11 9

Typeset and printed in Great Britain by
Toptown Printers Limited
Vicarage Lawn, Barnstaple, North Devon
England

Photographic processing by C.J.P. Photographic
Exeter, Devon

Most of the photographs used to illustrate this title are reproduced courtesy of the Regimental Headquarters of the Gloucestershire Regiment. The Regiment has a fine museum at Custom House, Commercial Road, Gloucester, which has been the subject of considerable rebuilding, extension and improvement of late, and is once again open to the public. The author wishes to thank the staff of the Regimental Headquarters and museum for their help in the preparation of this publication.

Above: Captain H.C. Woodcock of the 3rd Volunteer Battalion, Gloucestershire Regiment, c. 1905. The uniform was drab (khaki) with red facings, silver lace and green hat feathers.

Below: A group of B Company, 2nd Volunteer Battalion, Gloucestershire Regiment in 1901. The uniforms were rifle green and were similar to those worn by the 1st (City of Bristol) Volunteer Battalion.

The Gloucestershire Regiment

Origins

In the spring of 1694 there was raised in Portsmouth "by Beat of Drum or otherwise" a regiment of foot commanded by Colonel John Gibson, the city's Lieutenant Governor. So came into being Gibson's Regiment, a unit that subsequently became De Lalo's, Mordaunt's, Windsor's, Barrell's, Price's and Bragg's before becoming the 28th Foot in 1742.

In 1756 the 3rd Foot, the "Buffs", raised a second battalion, a unit which was reconstituted as the 61st Foot two years later. By a General Order of 1782 foot regiments were linked with counties for recruiting purposes, resulting in the 28th and the 61st becoming the "28th, or North Gloucestershire Regiment", and the "61st, or South Gloucestershire Regiment". For nearly a century both Regiments existed with these identities until, in 1881, the Army reforms of Edward Cardwell, Secretary of State for War, took away their numbers and re-named them the 1st and 2nd Battalions of the Gloucestershire Regiment.

At the same time the Royal South Gloucestershire Militia became the 3rd Battalion of the Regiment, the Royal North Gloucestershire Militia, the 4th. The 1st (City of Bristol) Gloucestershire Rifle Volunteers became the 1st (City of Bristol) Volunteer Battalion, The Gloucestershire Regiment and the 2nd Gloucestershire Rifle Volunteers became the 2nd Volunteer Battalion of the Regiment. Regimental Headquarters and Depot were at Horfield Barracks, Bristol.

It was with this organisation that the Gloucestershire Regiment entered the Twentieth Century but let it not be assumed that the shotgun wedding of the Cardwell reforms had been cheerfully accepted. Both the regular battalions continued to refer to themselves as the "28th" or the "61st" (usually written as "LXI"), whilst the issue as to who would and would not wear the "Back Number" of the "28th" gen-

India 1907. Sergeant Jarvis of the "28th" posing for the well-known watercolour painting by Major A.C. Lovett, the Gloucestershire Regiment. Note the "shorts" and 1903 bandolier equipment.

erated much argument. In this the new Regiment was not alone. All the old "Regiments of Foot" were jealous of their reputations and traditions, and the 28th and 61st had good reason to be. In the years since their respective formation, they had fought bravely in the great battles that forged the British Empire, a fact evidenced by the honours borne on their Colours. These were merged to be emblazoned on the Colours of the new Regiment to include:- "Egypt" and the Sphinx (from both former Regiments), "Ramilles", "Louisberg", "Guadaloupe, 1759", "Quebec, 1759", "Martinique, 1762", "Havannah", "St. Lucia, 1778", "Maida",

"Corunna", "Talavera", "Busaco", "Barrosa", "Albuhera", "Salamanca", "Vittoria", "Pyrenees", "Nivelle", "Nive", "Orthes", "Toulouse", "Peninsula", "Waterloo", "Chillianwallah", "Goojerat", "Punjaub", "Alma", "Inkerman", "Sevastopol", and "Delhi, 1857".

In the years to come, as the Gloucestershire Regiment, they were to add many more.

The Regiment in the 20th Century

Both regular battalions of the Regiment were sent to South Africa on the outbreak of the Boer War. The 1st Glosters arrived first, only

3

to be trapped in Ladysmith during the Boer siege. The "61st" landed later at Capetown and were involved in Lord Roberts' campaign which ended in the capture of Bloemfontein and Pretoria. The 4th Battalion were mobilised and sent to St. Helena. Many volunteers for active service came from the Volunteer Battalions of the Regiment. Whilst the war was at its height the formation took place in Bristol of a 3rd Volunteer Battalion of the Gloucestershire Regiment.

The "61st" were the last battalion of the Regiment to quit South Africa in 1904. Left behind were the graves of 350 officers and men of the Regiment who lost their lives in the war against the Boers — a war that added four more Battle Honours to the Regiment's list.

Lessons learned in the South African War brought about many changes in British Army organisation, training, equipment and weapons in the post-war years. As far as the Gloucestershire Regiment was concerned, the changes in organisation amounted to the 3rd Battalion becoming a Special Reserve unit, the 4th Battalion being disbanded, whilst the 1st Volunteer Battalion took over its number as the 4th (City of Bristol) Battalion, the Gloucestershire Regiment in the newly-created Territorial Force. The 2nd and 3rd Volunteer Battalions were re-numbered as the 5th and 6th Battalions of the Regiment in the same organisation.

At this time the "28th" were in India and the "61st" in England. In 1910 the 1st Battalion came home after 17 years overseas and the 2nd Battalion went to Malta until 1913 and then to China. This, then, was the disposition of the Gloucestershire Regiment at the outbreak of the Great War.

The record of the battalions of the Regiment, Regular, Territorial and Service, in that terrible conflict was as follows:-

1st Battalion. Served in France and Flanders with the 1st (Regular) Division.

2nd Battalion. Served in France and Flanders and in Macedonia in the 27th (Regular) Division.

England c. 1901. Officers from the volunteer battalions pose in active service uniform and equipment before taking ship for South Africa to reinforce the regular battalions of the Glosters fighting in the war against the Boers. Note the mixture of serge and drill clothing, the mixed khaki and drab and the lack of back badges.

3rd (Special Reserve) Battalion. Served in the United Kingdom as a Training Unit.

(The Territorial Force Battalions formed second and third-line units on the outbreak of war.)

1/4th (City of Bristol) Battalion. Served in France and Flanders and in Italy with the 48th (South Midland) Division — T.F.

1/5th Battalion. Served in France and Flanders and in Italy with the 48th (South Midland) Division — T.F. and the 25th Division (New Army).

1/6th Battalion. Served in France and Flanders and in Italy with the 48th (South Midland) Division — T.F.

2/4th Battalion. Served in France and Flanders with the 61st (2nd South Midland) Division — T.F.

2/5th Battalion. Served in France and Flanders with the 61st (2nd South Midland) Division — T.F.

2/6th Battalion. Served in France and Flanders with the 61st (2nd South Midland) Division — T.F.

3/4th, 3/5th and 3/6th Battalions.

Served in the United Kingdom as Reserve Battalions.

7th (Service) Battalion. Served in Gallipoli, Egypt, Mesopotamia and Persia with the 13th (New Army) Division.

8th (Service) Battalion. Served in France and Flanders with the 10th (New Army) Division.

9th (Service) Battalion. Served in France and Flanders and in Macedonia with the 26th (New Army) Division and the 66th (2nd East Lancs) Division — T.F.

10th (Service) Battalion. Served in France and Flanders with the 1st (Regular) Division.

11th (Reserve) Battalion. Served in the United Kingdom.

12th (Service) Battalion. (Bristol's Own). Served in France and Flanders and Italy with the 5th (Regular) Division.

13th (Service) Battalion (Forest of Dean) (Pioneers). Served in France and Flanders with the 39th (New Army) Division.

14th (Service) Battalion (West of England) (Bantams). Served in

Above: A group of the 3rd Glosters, England 1904. The former Royal South Gloucestershire Militia, the 3rd Bn were soon to become the Regiment's Special Reserve battalion. At left is a groom in "canvas" overalls, and beside him stands the Sergeant Major in Service Dress. The remainder are officers of the Battalion in various patterns of Service Dress, dark blue "patrols" and an undress frock coat.

Below: Tientsin, China, 1913. The full kit layout, left, and the daily kit layout of the 2nd Glosters. Note the "Boxes, soldier", (still in use in tropical stations fifty years later) alarm clocks, framed photos and certificates of education, and the many items of clothing and equipment familiar to soldiers for many years to come, especially the "knife, fork, spoon, razor, comb, lather brush, button stick and button brush" in the holdall.

Malta, 1913. The 2nd Glosters parade as for "full mobilisation" on the Floriana square. Note the eight-company organisation, relatively few mounted officers, bicycle orderlies, transport, stretcher bearers (band) and the two machine gun carts.

France and Flanders with the 35th (New Army) Division.

15th (Reserve) Battalion. Served in the United Kingdom.

16th (Reserve) Battalion. Served in the United Kingdom.

17th Battalion (T.F.). Served in the United Kingdom.

18th (Service) Battalion. Served in France and Flanders with the 16th (New Army) Division.

The service of these battalions gained for the Gloucestershire Regiment seventy-two Battle Honours.

The war over, demobilisation was a rapid affair with a return to the system of one regular battalion overseas and the other at home. The "61st" sailed for India in 1919 and, in the following year, the "28th" were sent to Ireland to "keep the peace". From here they followed a trail that led to Silesia, Cologne, and England before going to Egypt in 1928 on the return home of the 2nd Battalion. After three years in Egypt and one in Singapore the 1st Battalion moved to India and in 1938 they moved to Burma. Here they remained until the Japanese invaded that country in December 1941.

The overseas tour of the "61st" had culminated in an "emergency tour" of Shanghai in 1927. Their home tour was likewise interrupted when, in 1936, they were sent to Egypt.

Home again in 1937 they were stationed in Plymouth, from where they were mobilised for war in 1939.

The Territorial Battalions of the Regiment were reformed into the new Territorial Army of the early 1920s. In 1938 the 4th Glosters were "converted" to become the 66th Searchlight Regiment, Royal Artillery, and the 6th Glosters, by a similar process, became the 44th Battalion, Royal Tank Corps. Only the 5th Battalion remained as infantry and in 1938 they formed a second-line unit, designated the 7th Battalion. Thus, the outbreak of war in September 1939 found the Gloucestershire Regiment with one regular battalion in Burma, one regular battalion in the United Kingdom, a Territorial battalion mobilising and a second Territorial battalion in the process of formation. The record of these battalions and the battalions of the Regiments formed after the outbreak of war was as follows:-

The 2nd and the 5th Glosters were the first to see action in the Second World War, both going to France with the new British Expeditionary Force. Early in 1940 several regular battalions were "exchanged" to Territorial Divisions. The "61st" were one such unit, and they found themselves in the same Division as the 5th Battalion. Thus, both fought with the 48th Division as the

B.E.F. withdrew before the German onslaught of May 1940. After the Dunkirk evacuation both battalions were reformed in England, the 5th Glosters being lost to the Reconnaissance Corps in 1941. Four years later the "61st" went back to France with the 56th Independent Infantry Brigade and fought through the campaign in North West Europe (latterly with the 49th Division), to finish as part of the Berlin garrison after the German surrender.

The "28th" spent the war garrisoning Burma until the Japanese invasion of that country, after which it fell to their lot to conduct a fighting rearguard action from Rangoon to the Assam border, arriving at Kohima with only four officers and a fragment of the original battalion strength. After reinforcement the "28th" served with the 17th Indian Division, and, later the 8th Indian Division. The next Glosters in action against the Japanese were a wartime-raised battalion of the Regiment, the 10th.

Formed in 1940 the 10th Glosters had been "converted" to a tank regiment in 1942. Sent to India they were ordered to "revert" to the infantry role, posted to the 36th Division, and early in 1944 went into action against the Japanese in the Arakan. Later in the year they were flown in to Myitkyina with the

(continued on page 18)

24 battalions of the Gloucestershire Regiment served during the Great War and of those 15 fought in "France and Flanders". The experience of warfare in the mud and the trenches of the Western Front was, therefore, shared by most officers and men of the Glosters. 8,100 members of the regiment lost their lives in the years 1914 to 1918.

The photograph above shows a typical trench scene of 1918. At right are the Commanding Officer and Second-in-Command of the 2/6th Glosters (183 Brigade, 61st South Midlands Division) prior to the battalion's departure to the Western Front in June 1916. The patches on their sleeves were blue. The 61st were the "second line" to the 48th South Midland Division, both being Territorial formations. The 1/4th and 1/6th Glosters served in 144 Brigade of the 48th Division alongside the 1/7th and the 1/8th Worcesters. Officers and men from all four battalions formed the 144th Light Trench Mortar Battery pictured below, "after the battle" on the 29th July 1916. Note the blue grenade of the mortarman worn on right sleeves. By 1918 each "L.T.M.B." was operating eight "light", 3-inch, Stokes mortars, weapons capable of throwing a 10lb 11oz (4.8 kg) bomb a maximum of 710 yards.

COLOUR PLATE A

The principal figure opposite depicts a Corporal "bomber" of 'A' Company, 1/5th Glosters in 1915. He prepares a number 12 "hairbrush" grenade for throwing and wears a set of pouches containing ten number 5 "Mills" grenades. Note the company colour worn on the right shoulder, "bomber's" grenade, and Imperial Service badge. The latter badge, shown in detail below, was worn by pre-war Territorials who had volunteered for service overseas in time of war. The photograph at left shows a group of 1/5th Glosters in April, 1916.

At centre is a Private of the 7th (Service) Battalion, the Gloucestershire Regiment, Mesopotamia, 1918. The 7th Glosters served with the 13th Division and won fame at Gallipoli.

The figure on the right depicts a Major of the 2nd Glosters, 27th Division, Macedonia, 1917. Note the yellow strip worn on the shoulders as the mark of the 27th Division, badges of rank and wound stripes. The slouch hat was a theatre issue.

Insignia shown on the colour plate includes (from top to bottom) the badge of the 4th Territorial Battalion, 1914; shoulder title of the 3rd Glosters, 1904; forage cap badge of a field officer, India 1910; overseas helmet badges, regular battalions 1899-1902; officers Service Dress collar badge, Territorial battalions 1908-c. 1920 (note the "T" for Territorial worn below and the "M" worn by Militia officers in the first decade of the century); other ranks collar badges worn until c. 1960, and the shoulder title of the 4th Glosters. Until it was granted to them to mark distinguished service in the Great War, the Territorial battalions were not permitted to wear the Back Badge, nor were they allowed the battle honour "Egypt" on the sphinx of their badges.

The badges on the photograph at left are:- 1. White metal "staybrite" Front Badge. 2. W.M. Front Badge. 3. W.M. 5th and 6th Territorial Battalion Front Badge 1908-c. 1920. 4. Gun metal Back Badge. 5. Officers bronzed Front Badge. 6. Bi-metal Back Badge 1920s-1930s. 7. Officer's bronzed Back Badge. 8. Officer's bronzed collar badges. 9. W.M. "staybrite" collar badges. 10. Regimental button, "staybrite", Queen's crown. 11. Regimental button, G.M., King's crown. 12. Officer's silver Front Badge — worn from the late 1950s until the early 1970s. T1. Regimental title, Territorial battalions 1921-1939. T2. Regimental title, 5th Glosters, 1908-c. 1920.

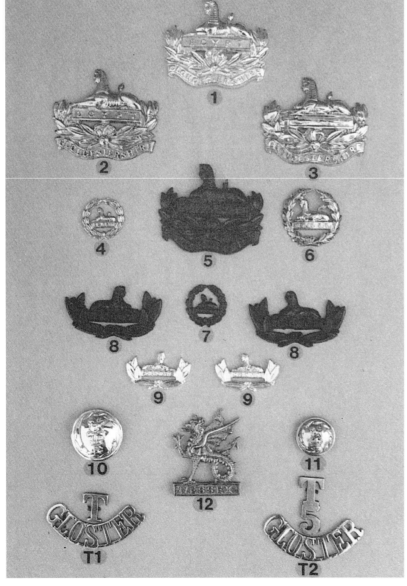

GLOSTER R.

GLOUCESTERSHIRE

GLOSTER

GLOSTER

EGYPT

COMMONWEALTH

COLOUR PLATE B

Due to the drafting of several battalions of the Regiment to other arms of the service, only four battalions of the Gloucestershire Regiment saw active service as infantry during the Second World War — the 1st, the 2nd, the 5th and the 10th. The central figure depicts a Private of the "61st" at the D-Day landings at Normandy. In addition to his other equipment he carries and operate a "Wireless Set No. 38". (The W.S. 38 was used for communications at company level. It weighed 12 pounds — 5.4 kgs — without its battery and had a range of less than 4 miles.) Note the Regimental title, 56th Independent Infantry Brigade sign, and infantry arm-of-service strip on his sleeve. (56 Brigade comprised the 2nd South Wales Borderers, 2nd Glosters and 2nd Essex — all of whom wore the Sphinx on their cap badges.) Note also his No. 4 rifle and bayonet, '37-pattern equipment, signal satchel and aerial case, and "Respirator, anti-gas, light." He wears an inflatable life jacket beneath his equipment. The top photograph on this page is of troops of the 56th Brigade landing on GOLD beach at 1100 hours on D-Day, 6th June 1944, in support of the brigade which had assaulted the beach three hours before.

The "28th" and the 10th Glosters fought in Burma. The 1st Battalion had the distinction of fighting rearguard on the retreat of 1942, whilst the 10th fought with the 36th Division in 1944/45. The figure at top, left depicts a Lieutenant of the "28th" in 1942, and that at top, right a Private of the 10th in 1945, by which time jungle green uniforms had replaced khaki drill. The bottom photograph on this page was taken in March 1942 and shows a position of the 1st Battalion whilst holding the railway at Toungoo.

Five battalions of the Glosters served in the United Kingdom during the war. The figure at bottom, left depicts an N.C.O. of one of them — the 7th Battalion. Note his wartime "plastic" cap badges and the insignia of the 61st Division. Below this figure is the Divisional sign of the 48th Division (in which both the "61st" and the 5th Battalions served for a time), the shoulder title adopted in late-1943, the title in use for a time from June 1943, the "tally" of the 44th Royal Tank Regiment (ex-6th Glosters) and the title worn on Battledress from 1939 to 1943. (It was also worn with tropical uniform for some time after 1943.)

The figure at bottom, right depicts a Major of the Regiment c. 1950. Note the gold wire badges worn by officers and warrant officers (Back Badge shown below), titles worn with ends "rounded", and the formation sign of the Wessex Brigade group of regiments. (An organisation for training and manning including the Glosters and five other infantry regiments from "Wessex".)

Below are the formation signs worn by the 1st Glosters in Korea; the 29th Independent Brigade Group and the 1st Commonwealth Division. Shown also are two (American) versions of the badge of the Presidential Unit Citation. (British versions of this insignia are shown in the photograph (centre) on this page.) Shown also are the Battledress title, two versions of the bullion Front Badge, the bullion Front Badge worn from the late-1950s until the early-1970s and the current bullion Back Badge.

11

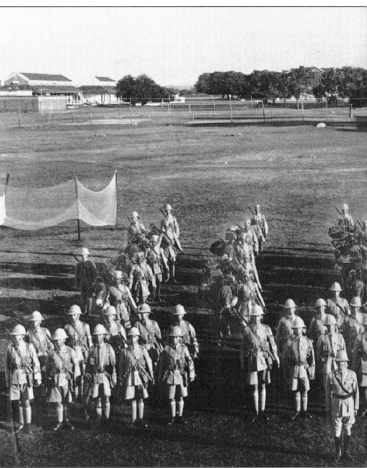

1918-1939. The years between the Great War and the Second World War saw the British Army return to the main duty of policing 1930s), and in 1938 and 1939 serious preparation was made for the war with Hitler's Germany, by then seen to be inevitable. Th company ready to march. Guns, tripods, ammunition boxes, etc. are on mule pack, the animals being handled by Indian muletee

By 1938 the 2nd Glosters were stationed in Plymouth where the photograph at bottom, centre was taken. In 1937 the Glosters w Glosters had three machine gun companies and an anti-tank company. The photograph shows the types of transport and weapc rifle; Bren l.m.g.; motor-cycle, carrier and 15cwt truck.

In 1936 the 2nd Glosters were part of a force "rushed" to Egypt because of the tension between Britain and Italy over Mussolini

The Colonel of the Regiment at this time (in fact from 1931 to 1947) was Brigadier-General A.W. Pagan, D.S.O. pictured left. An mid-1915 until March 1918, when he was appointed to the command of a Brigade. Author of "Infantry", the story of the 1st Glo Glosters, Lt-Colonel Pagan was wounded in the eye and marked for evacuation to England. The story goes that he walked out of

"Mechanisation" — the changeover from animal transport to mechanical transport — took place at this time (mainly in the late-
●hs at the centre of these pages show the Glosters undergoing these changes. Above, 2nd Glosters India 1927. The machine gun

to convert to a machine gun regiment (an order that was rescinded in June 1939). As M.G. battalion of the 3rd Division the 2nd
a M.G. battalion in 1938 including the 2-pounder anti-tank gun on an early-type carriage; Vickers machine gun; Boys anti-tank

●. The sentry at Mersa Matruh, right, may or may not have been a Private Canute. Note the large back badge.
erved with distinction for 35 years, Pagan was with the 2nd Glosters in the South African War and commanded the "28th" from
●18, the Brigadier-General went on to become Assistant Commandant of the School of Infantry. In 1916, whilst commanding 1st
in dressing-gown and "canvas shoes", hitch-hiked back to his battalion, and in defiance of all authority, continued to lead them.

COLOUR PLATE C

The 1950s saw the 1st Glosters, by now the "28th/61st" and the only regular battalion of the Regiment, committed to active service in many parts of the world, interspersed with duties at home and in B.A.O.R. The war in Korea was followed by a tour as Demonstration Battalion at the School of Infantry with the Battalion later embarking on a "Cook's tour" which took in operations against the Mau Mau in Kenya, riots in Bahrein and the "emergency" caused by EOKA nationalism in Cyprus. A two-year tour of Germany brought this active decade to a close.

The principal figure on this plate depicts a light mortar "number 1" in the Korean winter of 1950/51. He loads a round of smoke into his 2 inch mortar. Note his U.S. Army pile cap, Battledress with "windproof" trousers and smock (the last item rolled and tucked into his webbing), F.P. boots, '44-pattern webbing, woollen scarf, gloves and mittens. Two good conduct badges/stripes and ribbons for service in the Second World War mark him as a reservist recalled for the Korean War.

The top photograph on this page shows a group of officers of 1st Glosters and the Chief of the Imperial General Staff, Field Marshall Viscount Slim of Burma, at Colchester prior to embarkation for Korea — September 1950. With the Field Marshall are, left to right, Lt-Colonel, J.P. Carne, Captain A.H. Farrar-Hockley, M.C. and Captain P.W. Weller. Lt-Colonel Carne was to win both the Victoria Cross and a Distinguished Service Order in the months ahead. Captain Farrar-Hockley, then Adjutant, was to go on to become a General, Colonel of the Regiment and Colonel Commandant of the Parachute Regiment. In the photograph at centre can be seen a patrol of the 1st Glosters clearing a Korean hillside. Note their American pile caps and windproof clothing.

The remaining two figures on the colour pate are taken from the 1st Gloster's tour of duty in Cyprus, 1957-58. Stationed in Nicosia, the Battalion spent much of its time on "Internal Security" — guarding vital points and riot control. The figure at left illustrates the uniform and equipment worn in the cooler Cyprus weather. Note the black-painted helmet with Back-Badge transfer, '44-pattern equipment; the original trial F.N. self-loading 7.62 mm rifle, Light A.G. respirator and "C.W.W." boots. The photograph at the bottom of this page shows Support Company of the 28th/61st in the Turkish quarter of the old city of Nicosia, 1957.

At this time companies of the Battalion participated in operations in the mountain and rural areas of Cyprus. Typical dress and equipment for mountain operations are worn by the figure at right. Note his windproof clothing, Bergen rucksack and Mk V Sten machine-carbine.

Plate C

COLOUR PLATE D

Shown on this plate are a number of items of uniform and certain dress distinctions peculiar to the Gloucestershire Regiment since the Second World War.

The wearing of scarlet chevrons with tropical uniform was continued until recent times. The main figure, a Sergeant of the 1960s, demonstrates this practice. Note also his Small Arms Instructor's badge — crossed rifles — above the chevrons, pin-on U.S. Presidential Unit Citation badges, brass "GLOSTER" titles, and the yellow-topped hosetops introduced about 1957. At this time chevrons were worn on the right arm only. (At the foot of this column is a photograph of the chevrons, Regimental Signals Instructor's badge and citation worn by the author.) This form of uniform is shown in the photograph at the bottom of this page. Note the very light-khaki uniforms worn by the officers, including Lt-Colonel P.C.S. Heidenstam — then Commanding Officer. (Uniform worn in the field at this time was less formal, as evidenced by the photograph of the 1st Glosters Mortar Platoon! Top, right.)

In the 1960s officers adopted a black pullover for barrack wear. This is shown being worn with the Regimental field service "sidecap" by the other figure on the plate — a Second-Lieutenant. A reversion to the traditional badge of the Regiment in the early 1970s saw a new design of gold-wire Front Badge for officers. This is shown at the bottom of the plate, beside an example of the Regimental stable belt.

Insignia shown includes (from top to bottom) the "KK" formation sign of the 49th Brigade (Kenya), that of the 12th Brigade (B.A.O.R.), the panther's head of the 19th Brigade (U.K.), the Berlin Brigade's red circle and the battleaxe of the 11th Armoured Brigade (B.A.O.R.). Below this is the insignia worn on the left sleeve of Battledress by the Bristol company of the 5th Glosters prior to the disbandment of the Battalion and the 43rd (Wessex) Division in 1967. Men of the Machine Gun Platoon of this fine Battalion are shown in 1954 in the centre photograph on this page.

rest of the 36th Division to strike south for Mandalay. After a series of battles the Battalion crossed the Irrawaddy in January 1945 to fight their last major battle at Myitson. In May the 10th Glosters were flown to Mandalay from where they returned to India to be disbanded in December 1945.

The remaining wartime battalions of the Regiment were the 7th, the 8th (Home Service), the 9th (Garrison), the 11th and the 70th (Young Soldiers). All served in the United Kingdom, mainly in defence, training and reinforcement roles.

The nature of the fighting during the Second World War switched the emphasis from infantry to other arms. Three armoured, one reconnaissance and two artillery units were formed on what had been battalions of the Gloucestershire Regiment, leaving only four battalions to see action as infantry. Nevertheless, they won a further twenty Battle Honours for the Regiment.

Victory in Europe and against Japan was followed by rapid demobilisation and a further cut-back in infantry. In 1948 the 1st and 2nd Battalions were ordered to amalgamate (ceasing to be the "28th" and the "61st" sixty-seven years after the abolition of these titles — becoming instead the "28th/61st") and the post-war reconstruction of the Territorial Army called for only one T.A. battalion of the Regiment — the 5th.

The "61st" had gone to the West Indies in 1946 whilst the "28th" remained in India, where it was reduced to a cadre. After amalgamation the "28th/61st" returned home in 1949, and in 1950 mobilised as part of the 29th Independent Brigade Group for the war in Korea. Like the other units of the 29th Brigade, the 1st Glosters shed most of their National Servicemen, made up strength with Regular Army reservists recalled from civil life, and sailed for Korea in October of that year.

The part played by the 1st Glosters in the battle at the Imjin River in April 1951, has passed into legend. (Overshadowing the assault and capture of Hill 327, on February

Drum Major P.R. Brown of the 1st Battalion, India, 1935. In 1945 he was to win the Distinguished Conduct Medal.

16th.) The strength of the Battalion on April 22nd was 917 all ranks. On April 25th only 234, 46 of them survivors of the fighting echelon that had been cut off and surrounded at Solma-Ri, answered the roll-call. The rest were dead or were being marched to captivity in North Korea.

The press, in their customary manner, went over the top in their reportage of the battle, coining one of the less-acceptable nicknames the Regiment has borne — "The Glorious Glosters". But perhaps the finest accolade came from the Commander of the 29th Brigade, Brigadier Brodie, when he wrote

"Nobody but the Glosters could have done this." The Americans awarded the 1st Glosters the Presidential Unit Citation.

Reformed, the Battalion fought on in Korea for the rest of the year before returning to the United Kingdom. The captives of the Imjin battle were released after the 1953 armistice and the Regiment added three more Battle Honours to its list.

In 1955 the "28th/61st" were off on another tour of Britain's overseas trouble spots. 1958 saw them in B.A.O.R., from where they returned to England in 1960. In 1962 they set off for what was

(continued on page 24)

Military music and ceremonial, important factors in the building and maintenance of esprit-de-corps in the British Army, have always been performed to high standards in the Glosters. The top photograph shows the Corps of Drums of the 5th Glosters (T.A.) leading the battalion as they march past the Minister of War, Mr. Hore-Belisha. Annual camp, 1939. At centre, left, the Colours of the "28th" are trooped on the parade to mark the amalgamation of the 1st and 2nd Battalions. Jamaica, 1948. At centre, right, the Colour party of the "28/61st" parades whilst with the United Nations Force, Cyprus 1982. Below, left, the Queen's Colour of the "28th/61st" is marched past at Osnabruck, B.A.O.R., on Back Badge Day, 21st March 1959. Note the "Solma-Ri" streamer of the United States' Presidential Unit citation flying from the top of the pike. Bandmaster to the 1st Glosters in Berlin, 1968, was W.O.I. Don Carson, pictured below, right.

1939-1945. Both the 1st and the 10th Glosters served in Burma in the Second World War. The 1st in the desperate retreat to the borders of India and the 10th in the reconquest of Burma. At top, left, Private Fields of the "28th" smashes electrical equipment before the withdrawal from Yenangyaung, April 1942. At top, right, a truckload of men of the 10th Glosters, Burma, January 1945. At centre, right an officer of the 10th displays a captured Japanese sword, Burma 1945. At centre, left, a group of officers and senior ranks of the 10th Battalion are seen at Poona, India, after the Japanese surrender. Note N.C.O.s badges of rank worn on shoulder straps. Below, left, are the officers of 'C' Company 2nd Glosters, Devon 1941. The company commander, Major P.C.S. Heidenstam, went on to become a Brigadier and Colonel of the Regiment. The 4th Glosters were "converted" to the 66th Searchlight Regiment in 1938 but clung resolutely to regimental dress distinctions (below, right) and the celebration of Back Badge Day.

The Korean War 1950-53. The 1st Glosters went to Korea with the 29th Brigade and served there from late-1950 until relieved by the 1st Welch in late-1951. Their finest hour was undoubtedly the battle to stem the Chinese crossing of the Imjin river, 22nd-25th April 1951. Cut off, the battalion fought to the end, losing 63 men killed and over six hundred to captivity in North Korea. (Within eight days a new battalion had been formed and was operational.) Top, left, 1st Glosters and tanks of the 8th Hussars advance to contact, February 1951. Top, right, Padre Sam Davies, chaplain to the 1st Glosters conducts a service before the Imjin battle. Centre, ringed by their captors, survivors of the Imjin fight rest on their march north. Below, left, some of the 46 officers and men who reached the safety of their own lines after the battle. Below, right, 1953. Lt-Colonel J.P. Carne, V.C., D.S.O. with officers and N.C.O.s of the Glosters on arrival in England after their release from captivity.

Top, left, Back Badge Day, Swaziland, 1966. Presentation of Swazi battleaxes, etc., to the 1st Glosters. Lt-Colonel H.L.T. Radice M.B.E. — then commanding — receives the weaponry. Top, right, B.A.O.R., 1971. 1st Glosters 120 mm WOMBAT anti-tank detachment takes post. Left, Libya, 1962. Members of the Signal Platoon, 1st Glosters, operating a "Station Radio No. 62" in manpack. Below, led by 'A' Company, the 1st Glosters march through the city of Bristol with "bayonets fixed, drums beating and Colours flying". The occasion for the exercising of these privileges was the return of the battalion from the first operational tour of Northern Ireland in 1969/70.

The Colonel-in-Chief of the Gloucestershire Regiment is H.R.H. the Duke of Gloucester, seen at top, left, firing a G.M.P.G. on a visit to the 1st Glosters. The present Colonel of the Regiment is Lt-General Sir John Waters, K.C.B., C.B.E. seen in the photograph above, chatting to one of the regiment's Army Cadets.

Recent activities of the 1st Glosters have found them in Gibraltar in 1985 (top, right) and Northern Ireland (right). Below, armoured personnel carriers of the battalion take part in the Allied Forces Day parade, Berlin 1987.

thought to be a prize posting, three years in a now-peaceful Cyprus. The peace, however, was broken in late-1963 when civil war between the Greek and Turkish populations errupted. The 1st Glosters were in the thick of it holding the ring until the arrival of the United Nations "peacekeeping" contingents.

From England in 1965 the "28th/61st" was sent to Swaziland to underpin a police force that was undergoing reorganisation, after which the Battalion moved to Berlin for garrison duties. In 1966 the government of the day saw fit to virtually disband the existing Territorial Army. With it went the 5th Glosters, leaving only the 1st Battalion to represent the Regiment.

It was from Berlin, in 1969, that the 1st Glosters moved for its first tour of Northern Ireland, experiencing the first heady days of welcome before the I.R.A. became active. There were to be many more tours of the troubled province. Perhaps more agreeable have been the subsequent tours of B.A.O.R., Berlin, Belize and Cyprus, and the trips for training to places such as Canada.

The present day finds the 1st Battalion, the Gloucestershire Regiment, ("28th/61st") in fine fettle and high morale as it looks forward to celebrating 300 years of its existence in 1994.

Customs and Traditions

The Back Badge — The origins of this distinction are something of a mystery. It is known that the 28th took to wearing a plate inscribed "28th" at the back of their caps to commemorate the battle of Alexandria (where they fought back to back) and this practice received official approval in 1830. The number was replaced by the present badge after the 1881 reforms, after which the history of the badge has been noted.

Nicknames — "The Old Braggs" — after Phillip Bragg, twenty five years Colonel of the 28th. "The Silver-tailed Dandies" — a reference to the lace on the coats of officers of the 61st. "The Slashers" — after a Montreal magistrate lost an ear to a party of the 28th in 1764. Later for the conduct of the 28th at the battle of White Plains, New York. "The Flowers of Toulouse" — after the dead of the 61st on the field of Toulouse, 1814. "The Back-Numbers". "The Fore and Afts".

Regimental Music — This includes "The Kinnegad Slashers" and "The Highland Piper" as the former marches of the old 28th and 61st and "The Young May Moon" to which the 28th marched off to Quatre Bras and Waterloo.

Regimental Days — The anniversary of the battle of Alexandria (1801) — Back Badge Day — is always celebrated on, or near, the 21st March. Lately, the anniversaries of the battles of Salamanca and the Imjin have also been celebrated.